Martin Luther King Jr.

JOSH GREGORY

Children's Press®
An Imprint of Scholastic Inc.
New York Toronto London Auckland Sydney
Mexico City New Delhi Hong Kong
Danbury, Connecticut

Content Consultant
James Marten, PhD
Professor and Chair, History Department
Marquette University
Milwaukee, Wisconsin

Library of Congress Cataloging-in-Publication Data
Gregory, Josh.
  Martin Luther King Jr. / by Josh Gregory.
     pages cm. — (A true book)
  Includes bibliographical references and index.
  Audience: Grades 4–6.
  ISBN 978-0-531-21194-6 (library binding : alk. paper) — ISBN 978-0-531-21208-0 (pbk. : alk. paper)
  1. King, Martin Luther, Jr., 1929–1968—Juvenile literature. 2. African Americans—Biography—
Juvenile literature. 3. Civil rights workers—United States—Biography—Juvenile literature. 4.
Baptists—United States—Clergy—Biography—Juvenile literature. 5. African Americans—Civil
rights—History—20th century—Juvenile literature. I. Title.
  E185.97.K5G75 2014
  323.092—dc23 [B]   2014030979

**Front cover: King in the National Mall in
Washington, D.C., during the March on Washington**

**Back cover: King giving the "I Have a Dream"
speech during the March on Washington**

Find the Truth!

Everything you are about to read is true *except* for one of the sentences on this page.

Which one is **TRUE**?

T or F   Martin Luther King Jr. was originally named Michael King Jr.

T or F   Martin Luther King Jr. believed that violence should be used to fight racism.

Find the answers in this book.

3

Contents

THE **BIG** TRUTH!

The March on Washington

King's actions inspired people around the nation to begin their own civil rights protests.

4 Far From Finished

What did King accomplish during his final years? 33

King's speeches often drew thousands of people.

5

Martin Luther King Sr. was pastor at the Ebenezer Baptist Church for four decades.

CHAPTER 1

Growing Up

On January 15, 1929, Michael and Alberta King welcomed a son into the world. They named him Michael King Jr. The Kings were a very religious family. Michael Sr. was the pastor of a large church in Atlanta, Georgia. When Michael Jr. was about five years old, his father changed both their names to Martin Luther King, in honor of the religious leader Martin Luther.

As a child, Martin often memorized long passages from the Bible.

Family Life

The Kings lived in a large home in one of Atlanta's wealthiest African American neighborhoods. Other relatives lived nearby. The family enjoyed a close-knit, loving relationship.

As a child, Martin Jr. enjoyed reading and playing sports. He also spent a lot of time studying the Bible and listening to his father deliver sermons at church.

Martin had an extremely close relationship with his grandmother.

Martin (front, right) poses for a photo with his parents, grandmother, brother, and sister.

8

Everything from waiting rooms to drinking fountains was segregated in the South during King's childhood.

A Segregated Nation

During the time Martin Luther King was growing up, **segregation** was legal. Black and white people were kept separate in businesses, services, and public places. For example, they used separate entrances, restrooms, and seating areas. Separate hospitals, schools, and other institutions were run for white people and nonwhite people. These segregated spaces were far from equal. The facilities black people used were often run-down or dirty.

Black people often faced difficulties trying to cast their votes in southern states.

Dealing With Racism

King encountered racism from a very young age. Racism existed across the United States, but it was especially powerful in the South. Black people were treated as inferior, often limited to lower-paying jobs and not allowed to live in white neighborhoods. Decades earlier, white legislators had passed laws to keep black people from voting. This gave the black population no power in government. Physical danger was a constant threat, as beatings and **lynchings** occurred without any legal consequences to the attackers.

School Days

King began attending college when he was just 15 years old. He enrolled at Morehouse College, a black school in Atlanta that his father had attended. There, he developed his public speaking skills and studied a variety of topics. He also began to think more about ways that he could help fight racism and segregation.

King (front row, third from left) listens carefully during a lecture at Morehouse College.

A Religious Education

King considered several career paths during his time at Morehouse. He eventually decided to follow in his father's footsteps and become a pastor. In 1948, he began preaching at his father's church. Later that year, he enrolled at Crozer Theological Seminary, a religious school in Pennsylvania. There, he learned about the life and teachings of Mahatma Gandhi.

As a pastor, King built close relationships with the people in his community.

Mahatma Gandhi

During the early 20th century, Mahatma Gandhi led the people of India in their battle for independence from Great Britain. He did not believe in using violence to achieve his goals. Instead, he encouraged his followers to peacefully disobey unfair British laws. He organized marches and other events to protest British rule. Gandhi's peaceful methods of resistance were a major influence on King.

The Kings celebrated their marriage on June 18, 1953.

Coretta Scott was studying music when she met Martin.

Marriage and a New Job

After graduating from Crozer, King decided to pursue a doctorate degree. In 1951, he began studying at Boston University in Massachusetts. While in Boston, he began dating a young woman named Coretta Scott. They were married in June 1953. Just a few months later, King finished his classes at Boston University. In early 1954, he and his wife moved to Montgomery, Alabama, where he began a job as a pastor.

A Change in the Air

King had lived in the north Boston area for several years. He knew it would be difficult to return to the more widespread racism and segregation of the South. However, changes were soon to come. In May 1954, the U.S. Supreme Court declared segregation in public schools to be **unconstitutional**. While this ruling did not end segregation completely, it marked the beginning of a major movement for **civil rights**.

The Supreme Court's decision in *Brown v. Board of Education* helped begin an era of civil rights progress for African Americans.

Working as a pastor
helped King become a
magnetic speaker.

Starting a Movement

In Montgomery, King's remarkable speaking skills and thoughtful sermons made him popular as a pastor. He became active in the local branch of the National Association for the Advancement of Colored People (NAACP), a major civil rights organization. He and his fellow members discussed plans for convincing the city's black population to join together and fight for change.

King's church in Montgomery was called the Dexter Avenue Baptist Church.

Staying Put

Montgomery's local laws required black people to give up their seats when white people wanted to sit down on crowded buses. On December 1, 1955, a woman named Rosa Parks was riding a full bus home after a long day of work. When the white driver demanded that Parks give up her seat to a white passenger, she refused. As a result, she was arrested.

Rosa Parks was a longtime member of the NAACP.

Rosa Parks's brave resistance helped start a movement in Montgomery.

During the bus boycott, many black people walked to work and school instead of relying on public transportation.

The Boycott Begins

A group of **activists** began organizing a **boycott** of Montgomery's bus system in response to the unfair treatment of black passengers such as Rosa Parks. They had heard King speak and knew he would be a **charismatic** leader, so they convinced him to join the effort. The group set up a carpool system throughout the city so people could get around without riding buses. Soon, the buses were practically empty on many routes. The bus company began losing money.

Buses were left almost completely empty during the boycott.

A Long Battle

Racial tension flared up in response to the bus boycott. As the leader of the protest, King was the target of many attacks from angry white people. He and his family received a constant flow of hate mail and threatening phone calls. A stick of dynamite was left by someone on his front porch and exploded. At one point, the Montgomery police arrested King. In spite of these difficulties, he did not back down.

Victory at Last

About a year after the boycott began, the U.S. Supreme Court declared that segregation in buses was unconstitutional. King and the other activists were overjoyed. Their hard work and sacrifice had paid off. However, King knew that there were many obstacles left to overcome. With his newfound fame and the lessons he had learned during the boycott, he began planning to expand the movement even further.

King and other protesters were among the first to ride on Montgomery's buses after achieving victory with their boycott.

21

King removes his shoes
before approaching a shrine
to Gandhi in India.

CHAPTER 3

The National Stage

In 1957, King joined together with other black religious leaders to form the Southern Christian Leadership Conference (SCLC). With the SCLC, King planned to help people across the country organize peaceful protests. He began giving speeches throughout the nation. His fame soon spread around the world. He traveled to Africa and India, where he met with Gandhi's followers.

King met with India's top government officials on his trip.

Sitting Down

As King and the SCLC spread their message, people in many cities began staging protests of their own. One took place in early 1960 in Greensboro, North Carolina. A group of black students sat at a "whites only" lunch counter and refused to leave until they received service. Similar sit-ins began happening in dozens of other cities. King was briefly jailed in October 1960 for joining a group of students at an Atlanta sit-in.

From left to right: Joseph McNeil, Franklin McCain, Billy Smith, and Clarence Henderson were among the protesters who began the sit-in movement in Greensboro in February 1960.

Protesters in Chicago hold up signs outside a Woolworths store in protest of the company's policy of segregating its southern stores.

Off to Birmingham

By 1963, an organized nationwide civil rights movement was in full swing. Across the country, people were working to desegregate their cities one small step at a time. However, many white people firmly resisted any attempts to end segregation. One of the most segregated cities was Birmingham, Alabama. King and his allies chose it as their next big target.

King and fellow civil rights leader Ralph Abernathy were arrested in Birmingham on April 12, 1963.

A Rough Start

King helped organize a series of sit-ins, boycotts, marches, and other protests throughout Birmingham. He hoped that these activities would draw negative attention to Birmingham's local government and businesses, forcing them to change their ways. During the protests, King and many other activists were arrested and jailed.

Letter From Jail

While in jail, King read a newspaper article criticizing his methods. In response, King wrote a long letter. He explained, "One has not only a legal but a moral responsibility to obey just laws. Conversely [on the other hand], one has a moral responsibility to disobey unjust laws." The letter was published in magazines and as a short book, and it became one of the most effective and memorable texts of the civil rights movement.

King spent his time in jail composing the letter that would become one of his most widely read works.

Young and Brave

King was released from jail on April 20, 1963, just over a week after he had been arrested. Following his release, the protests began to ramp up. In early May, thousands of students joined the cause. Many of them were very young, but the Birmingham police showed them no mercy. They turned fire hoses and police dogs on all the protesters and sent hundreds of them to jail.

Birmingham police used brutal tactics in their attempts to control protesters.

Protesters dance and sing in Birmingham as police attempt to make them move.

A Big Win in Birmingham

Photos and reports of the harsh treatment of the protesters made headlines around the world. To avoid hurting the city's reputation any further, Birmingham leaders agreed to begin desegregation.

The news coverage brought nationwide attention to civil rights in the South. White and black people alike rallied behind King and his allies. In June, President John Kennedy announced that he would ask the U.S. Congress to pass a law outlawing all segregation once and for all.

The March on Washington

King and other civil rights leaders began planning a massive event. About a quarter of a million people gathered in Washington, D.C., on August 28, 1963.

A Stirring Speech

Near the Lincoln Memorial, the huge crowd listened to some of the movement's greatest leaders. King was the last speaker to step up to the microphone. In his strong voice, he delivered an emotional speech. In one of the most well-known passages, he said:

> *I have a dream that my four little children will one day live in a nation where they will not be judged by the color of their skin, but by the content of their character. . . . I have a dream that one day, down in Alabama . . . little black boys and black girls will be able to join hands with little white boys and white girls as sisters and brothers.*

King's powerful words rang out around the world, increasing support of new civil rights laws. His speech is remembered today as one of the greatest speeches ever delivered.

King stood behind President Lyndon B. Johnson as he signed the 1964 Civil Rights Act into law.

CHAPTER 4

Far From Finished

On July 2, 1964, the Civil Rights Act became law. The act was the greatest victory yet for King and the civil rights movement. It outlawed segregation throughout the country. It also added new legal protections to prevent **discrimination** by employers and to ensure voting rights.

For his role in such an important change, King was awarded the Nobel Peace Prize in 1964.

King also spoke out against U.S. involvement in the Vietnam War.

Young activists protest voting laws in Selma on February 5, 1965.

More than 400 people were arrested during the protests in Selma.

Problems at the Polls

Even with the new laws in place, local governments in the South found ways to prevent black people from voting. In early 1965, King traveled to Selma, Alabama, to begin a protest for stronger voting rights laws. He led several marches through the city. He was once again arrested, along with hundreds of fellow protesters.

After his release from jail, King helped organize a march from Selma to the state capital in Montgomery. The long march would demonstrate the activists' determination and bring public attention to their efforts. Hundreds of protesters gathered in Selma on March 7, 1965, to begin the march. However, the Alabama state police blocked their path and beat them with clubs. King had been preaching at his church in Montgomery. He was horrified to hear about the violence.

Police mercilessly beat protesters with clubs to prevent the march from Selma to Montgomery.

The Voting Rights Act

King personally led a second march a few days later. Once again, state police blocked the marchers. This time, King and his followers turned back to avoid violence. Mounting pressure from the rest of the nation soon forced the Alabama governor to relent. On March 21, King led thousands of protesters to Montgomery without police interference. The protest raised awareness of voting rights violations and led to the Voting Rights Act of August 1965.

Thousands of people followed King on the march to Montgomery.

King met with President Lyndon Johnson on March 18, 1966.

Heading North

Though discrimination was more openly practiced in the South, it affected black people throughout the country. In cities such as Los Angeles and Chicago, local laws made it hard for black people to move into white neighborhoods. This often forced them to live in poor, run-down areas. In 1966, King and his family moved to a poor black neighborhood in Chicago. There, he planned to draw attention to the city's unfair housing situation.

King speaks to a huge crowd at Chicago's Soldier Field.

Struggling in Chicago

In Chicago, King led marches and other peaceful protests as he had throughout the South. However, these demonstrations made little difference in the city's situation. Chicago's leaders argued that poverty and housing were not civil rights issues. In the face of such setbacks, many African Americans began embracing a different approach to fighting racism.

A New Approach

Leaders such as Malcolm X and Stokely Carmichael encouraged black nationalism over King's plan for **integration**. They argued that King's peaceful methods were not powerful enough to win truly equal treatment. Instead, black nationalists believed that black people should remain separate from white people. They would gain equality by increasing their own power in government and business. Black nationalists also believed that black people should fight back against violent attacks.

The Fight Against Poverty

In the following years, King focused heavily on battling poverty and winning rights for workers. He began planning another march on Washington, D.C. This one would address not only civil rights for black people but also the issue of poverty among all races.

In 1968, King's work brought him to Memphis, Tennessee. There, he planned to support a group of workers who were on **strike**.

King leads a march to support the striking workers in Memphis on March 28, 1968.

40

King's friends point in the direction of the shooter as King falls to the floor.

James Earl Ray eventually took back his confession and denied shooting King.

A Tragic Loss

On the evening of April 4, 1968, King walked out on the balcony of his hotel in Memphis. As he was talking with some fellow activists, a shot rang out. King was hit by a bullet. He was quickly taken to a hospital, but there was nothing the doctors could do. He died that evening. A white man named James Earl Ray later admitted to the murder.

Mourning a Hero

The nation was shaken by the loss of a great leader. Riots broke out in many cities, and dozens of people died in the chaos.

World leaders such as President Lyndon Johnson and Pope Paul VI expressed their sadness at the loss of this great man. King's funeral was held on April 9. Tens of thousands of mourners gathered in the streets outside his father's church in Atlanta to pay their respects.

Timeline of Martin Luther King Jr.

January 15, 1929
Martin Luther King Jr. is born in Atlanta, Georgia.

June 18, 1953
King marries Coretta Scott.

A Remarkable Legacy

Martin Luther King Jr. is remembered as one of the United States' greatest heroes. His inspiring leadership helped bring about some of the most important changes in the country's history. Thanks to his work, African Americans were able to make great strides forward in the battle against discrimination. As the struggle to win equal rights for all Americans continues today, King's contributions will never be forgotten. ★

April 1963
King and other activists are arrested and jailed in Birmingham, Alabama.

August 28, 1963
King delivers his "I Have a Dream" speech in Washington, D.C.

April 4, 1968
King is murdered in Memphis, Tennessee.

Number of people at the March on Washington:
Around 250,000

Number of times Martin Luther King Jr. was arrested: 30

Number of people who completed the march from Selma to Montgomery: Around 25,000

Number of black citizens of voting age in Selma, Alabama, in 1965: Around 15,000

Number of black citizens registered to vote in Selma, Alabama, in 1965: 335

Age at which Martin Luther King Jr. enrolled in college: 15

Did you find the truth?

Martin Luther King Jr. was originally named Michael King Jr.

Martin Luther King Jr. believed that violence should be used to fight racism.

Resources

Books

Colbert, David. *Martin Luther King Jr.* New York: Simon and Schuster, 2008.

Gormley, Beatrice. *Malcolm X: A Revolutionary Voice*. New York: Sterling Publishing, 2008.

McLean, Alan C. *Martin Luther King*. New York: Oxford University Press, 2008.

Zeiger, Jennifer. *The Civil Rights Movement*. New York: Children's Press, 2012.

Visit this Scholastic Web site for more information on Martin Luther King Jr.:

★ www.factsfornow.scholastic.com
Enter the keywords **Martin Luther King Jr.**

Important Words

activists (AK-tiv-ists) — people who work for some kind of social change

boycott (BOI-kaht) — a refusal to buy something or do business with someone as a punishment or protest

charismatic (kar-iz-MAT-ik) — having a powerful personal appeal that attracts a great number of people

civil rights (SIV-uhl RITES) — the individual rights that all members of a democratic society have to freedom and equal treatment under the law

discrimination (diss-crim-uh-NAY-shun) — unfair treatment of others based on age, race, gender, or other factors

integration (in-tuh-GRAY-shuhn) — the inclusion of people of all races

lynchings (LINCH-engs) — the killings of others, often by hanging, done by a lawless mob

segregation (seg-ruh-GAY-shuhn) — the act of separating people based on race, gender, or other factors

strike (STRIKE) — a refusal to go to work until an employer meets certain demands

unconstitutional (uhn-kahn-sti-TOO-shuh-nuhl) — not in keeping with the basic principles or laws set forth in the constitution of a state or country

Index

Page numbers in **bold** indicate illustrations.

About the Author

Josh Gregory writes and edits books for kids. He lives in Chicago, Illinois.